DENNIS WILE

**Dear Parent,**
Your child learns from the minute he is born. He is always learning. Each child learns at his own speed. Just as children do not begin to crawl, walk, or talk at the same time, neither do they learn at the same rate. Children differ from one another and within themselves as to the rate at which they learn.

It is important for you to know how children learn. In this way you can provide learning experiences at home which will help.

Remember that there are things too difficult for your child to learn at certain stages of his development. What he learns has to be based on what he already knows, and it depends a lot on his health and emotions.

It is important to remember that while your child is busy learning some things, he may learn other things slowly.

You are very important to your child's learning. Make it fun!

**Happy teaching!**

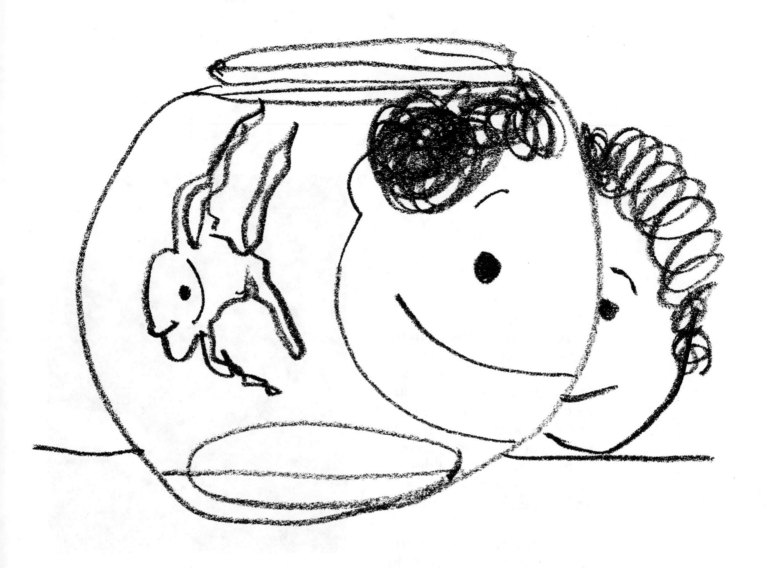

# Learning By Seeing

"Mom! Let me see! This is one of the most important ways I learn".

Mom says: "Look at the fish in the bowl! See how they swim! Their fins help them swim. Their tails help them move around and around. Up they go! Down they dive! See the bubbles in the water! Why do you think they are there?"

Yes! Seeing is important to your child's development. He learns many things with his eyes! And he wants to learn! Help him see many things. If not real things, then show him pictures. Ask him questions and COMPLIMENT him when he knows!

Later your child will be using his eyes to see words and to read them! You want him to be a good reader. It will help him if he knows the meaning and has seen many of the things he is reading about. You want him to be a good reader. Have his eyes checked. Even a small loss of sight can cause many reading problems.

# Learning By Listening

"Open your ears. Listen!"
Your child learns by hearing you talk. He learns many word meanings this way. He learns to understand things from hearing you talk.

He hears sounds from the street. And he will be able to tell if he hears a big truck, a small car, a motorcycle, a wagon, or a jet airplane.

Your child can tell you sounds made by animals. He hears differences in the "moo" of a cow, the "woof" of a dog, and the "quack" of a duck.

**And there are sounds in the house.** The drip of a leaking faucet, the ringing of a telephone, the sound of footsteps all train your child's ear for the more difficult sounds in reading.

When he begins to read, he will be able to pick out rhyming words and words that sound alike. His ability to hear will help him learn to use his ears in figuring out words in reading.

Help your child learn by **listening!**

# Learning By Smelling and Tasting

Children are always snooping around. And if they find anything that looks strange and they become curious about it, they usually stop to smell or taste it.

The smell of fresh bread in the oven or cookies baking "tickles" the taste buds and brings the children into the kitchen.

Knowledge of certain smells helps them avoid danger—smoke, gas, unfriendly animals.

Bath powder, perfume, lotions, and flowers smell fragrant. Yet onions, cinnamon, vinegar, and coffee neither taste nor smell pleasant to a child.

Although smelling and tasting are not as important to learning as the other senses are, they do have importance in the total learning of your child.

# Learning By Feeling

"Don't touch!"

Yes—many times children shouldn't touch certain things—things that are easily broken or which might hurt them.

But children learn many things through touching. Seeing and hearing are the two senses which are the main ways of learning. But we need to keep in mind that many children learn from the sense of touch.

A kitten is soft and fluffy. A dog may be smooth. A rabbit is furry. But many children are afraid of animals. There are many things to touch: the rough bark of a tree, the prickly feel of a pine cone, the soft feel of cotton, the slick feel of plastic, and the rough feel of sandpaper.

Your child begins to learn shapes—round, square, triangle—by touching and feeling. And they learn to touch and tell whether things are large or small.

Give your youngster the chance to feel things, and talk about these things while you are helping him develop many new word meanings.

# Doing And Learning

The more he does, the more he learns.

Doing is learning. When your child does something, he is using many of his senses. It may be a simple thing, such as putting toys away or wiping up a spill. It could be caring for a pet or a plant. It could be playing in the sand, mud, or snow—which is really exploring science.

Playing is doing also. **Your child learns much through play.** He practices skills. He imagines and creates. He learns to express himself and solve problems. He discovers things for himself.

So let your child do things.

THE BOWDOIN METHOD

# Moving And Learning

Children learn through movement. Little children need constant action. They should be able to walk and run well, walk up and down steps alone, walk on tiptoes, and jump with both feet. They need play that will help develop control of their large muscles—play such as running, walking, hopping, leaping, climbing, skipping, and balancing. Marching to music and dancing to music help the children improve their control.

After the large muscles are developed, your child needs things which will develop his fine muscles. He needs to hold a crayon and a big pencil properly. He needs to be able to sort things. Use egg cartons for sorting large buttons, bottle caps, macaroni, and pennies.

Learning to tie his shoe will develop fine muscles. Putting puzzles together is also excellent training, not only for the fine muscles, but for the mind as well.

Using pegboards, building with toys, using sewing cards, and stringing beads or macaroni all help in this development.

When your child is ready, give him opportunity for moving. The fine muscle movement will help his hand and eyes to work together, which will help him learn to read and write.

MACARONI

# Motivation and Learning

We don't usually like to do things we can't do well.

A child will perform better when he is stimulated and inspired. He must want to learn, and this comes from the home.

Mother can create interest by saying things like:

"You had so much fun looking at the pretty book." (The child will want to look again.)

"What a nice job you did with your picture!" (The child will want to do well the next time.)

"I know your teacher just loves your pretty writing." (The child will continue to take pride and try.)

A pat on the back, telling and showing daddy or grandmother will cause a child to want to learn and want to keep trying!

Like parent, like child!
Oh, yes! They want to be just like you! They want to talk as you talk, look as you look and act as you act!

And children learn to feel the way we feel. If we are kind, they usually are kind. If we are patient, they learn to be patient. If we feel good about others, they feel good about others!

And if we love they love. Then they will have a better chance to grow up to be good citizens, good neighbors.

How important it is that teachers and parents are good models!

# Imitation and Learning

# Repetition and Learning

"Mom, tell me again."

Your child learns by repetition. Learning is remembering, and this has to be developed by repeating things over and over again and again!

Have you noticed that your young child likes to hear you read the same story, or sing the same song, or play the same record over and over? He is asking for it. He may be remembering and learning something more each time. He is building new knowledge on the knowledge which he already has!

Older children need repetition, too. They need drill on many facts in order that they may remember them.

But there is a warning! Suppose the child is not repeating things right each time? He will discover some of this and correct himself. You will need to help him at times. Remember that bad things and wrong ways can be learned as well.

Very important things need to be repeated even after the child seems to have learned them. This increases memory even further. Yet there comes a time at which more trying is too discouraging or when more repetition gives no more learning. Then a wise parent will not insist beyond this point.

FUN is a key word when your child is repeating and learning! It should not be an unpleasant task. Do you remember the old saying, "One can lead a horse to water, but he can't make him drink!"? You want your child to remain willing to repeat.

# Curiosity and Learning

"Mamma, why?"

And sometimes we do not know all the answers. The questions are not all easy. But if he wonders, he wants to know.

We should answer questions the best we can—simply, but truthfully. If we do not know, we should not brush it aside. We should say, "We'll try to find out."

When a child is exposed to many things which "tickle" his senses, he will become more curious. He needs many experiences with touching, tasting, hearing, smelling and doing as you talk with him and work with him.

When you patiently stop to show your child an unusual rock or a beautiful leaf, to watch a butterfly flit from flower to flower, or to plant a seed in the garden, **you are teaching!** You are helping your child develop his curiosity. You are encouraging him to **want** to learn!

# Developing Good Habits

Learning involves the memory, but much doing takes little or no thinking. We call this habit.

As adults we may brush our teeth, set the alarm clock, shift gears in the car, and stop at the red light without thinking. In fact we do these things and many others often while thinking of something else. It would be very hard for us to have to think through each step.

Your child needs to develop (learn) many useful habits. Among these are brushing his teeth, putting up play things, going to bed willingly at the hour you set, waiting his turn, dressing himself, having acceptable table manners. And many other things which have value at once and carry over into later life.

Yes, of course it is important for your child to think about what he is doing. But there are many things your child will learn to do without thinking.

Help your child develop good habits, but only as he becomes mature enough for the task! If you **force** learning before there is readiness for it, harm can be done.

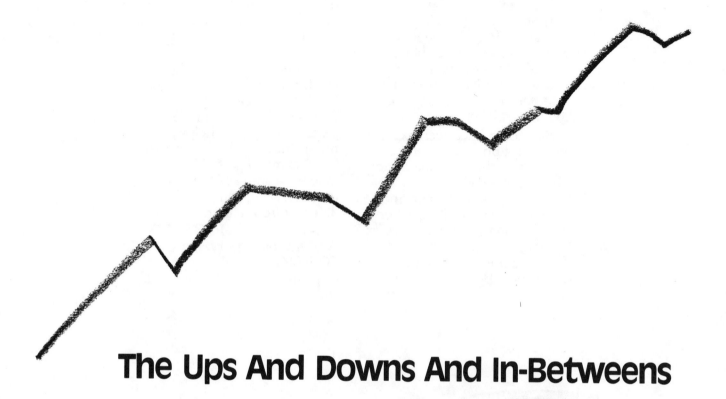

# The Ups And Downs And In-Betweens Of Learning

"My, how my child has learned! He is really learning fast!" But it may not always be so. Most children learn in spurts just as the parts of his body grow in spurts. Spurts make parents happy!

Next . . . No spurts! Could be. Your child may seem to be learning slower than others. He may be very slow. He may be at best on level ground, if not going downhill in his learning! He may have to stop a little while and "take in" what he has already learned. He may be getting ready for his next uphill climb!

This should not be cause for worry. It can be normal for your child and other children, too! It could be cause enough for you to make sure there are no physical problems. It could be cause enough to watch carefully for any emotional problems that he can't handle.

Just remember that your child's learning may be fast, level off, then get slower, then slow! And suddenly fast again! If you feel that your child is not learning and you think to yourself "I can't see a thing he has learned!" it is probably normal for him at this time. HAVE PATIENCE.

# Direction of Learning

Your child learns by seeing, hearing, smelling, tasting, and feeling the PARTS. He learns the words sweet, sour, bitter, and salty by tasting and later by seeing. He learns how to fit together the parts of a puzzle by sight and feel.

He should have such experiences. But do you remember the story of the three blind men who felt of the elephant? One felt of the elephant's side and thought it was a wall. Another felt of his leg and thought it was the trunk of a tree. The third felt of his trunk and thought it was a rope. By feeling of different parts each blind man came out with the wrong answer about what the elephant really was.

Sometimes your child should see the WHOLE first—then the PARTS. To see the silo and barn formed by the in-place parts of the puzzle helps when the picture is to be put together from its many parts. The cake may have some of the basic tastes—sweet, sour—but it is different from either.

Learning from PARTS TO WHOLE or from WHOLE TO PARTS—Both are good! Use this as you help your child learn.

# Associations And Near Misses

"Little doggie!" says the child who happens to see a sheep pass the window. Not right, but not all wrong either! It is an animal. It does have four legs. It is about the size of some dogs. It is the color of some dogs. He knows "dogs" but does not know "sheep."

"New learning"—words, pictures, things, and experiences need "old learning" as a starting point. The child should be encouraged to "guess" new meanings from what he has learned in the past—guess and correct with patient help from you!

There is a need for your child to draw upon what he already knows in order to help him learn the new things. The area of the known should, with help from you, be FOREVER EXPANDING!

# Punishment And Learning

"Mom, please don't hit me so hard!"

Punishment is at times effective, but its results are not always certain. Like some medicine, some bad side effects can result from the use of punishment. Sometimes the child will learn the thing you are wanting him to learn but at the same time he may learn a number of BAD THINGS! He can even learn to HATE at the same time.

Fair and mild punishment—none other is acceptable—is best used for stopping behavior that is dangerous to the child. When possible it may take the form of having the child correct something he has done—wipe up the milk, clean up the rug,

try to fix the thing he has broken, deny him of some privilege, try to repair the toy he has broken. All forms of punishment need to be explained to the child if he is old enough to understand WHY. With very young children the punishment should be given quickly, mildly if the behavior is to be corrected.

With an older child learning can take place in a warmer, happier atmosphere when the child **understands** why it is done. He may even help you with the kind of punishment he should have. (The child will usually "be harder" on himself than you would be).

In learning, there is a place and a use for mild punishment.

# Rewards And Learning

"Mom, what is that man giving the bird?" asks your child.

"A grasshopper I believe. That will cause the bird to come when he calls him next time", says mother.

This is the same with children. A reward—a word of deserved praise, a pat on the back, small favors are very likely to get the same desired behavior next time if it is not over done!

Rewards help the child develop a pattern of good behavior and good habits. But rewards of MONEY and THINGS are not felt to be the best ways of helping a child learn. Why? Because we often place our "stakes" too high for our children to reach! Often parents say "I'll give you a dollar for every 'A' you make". This may be fair for the child who has this ability, who finds it easy to learn. But children differ—and for some, making an "A" might come very hard!

If he strives TOO hard, if he is TOO anxious, if he is TOO afraid he will not please you, some bad things might happen along the way. PRESSURE to the point that he is extremely nervous, afraid, or insecure can result in poor mental health. This does not mean that you do not want from your child the VERY BEST he can give, but a wise parent will not harm his child by having him do things he can't do.

Rewards, however small, need to be repeated often. A one-time reward will not be enough to keep the learning "on track". They should not be used to cause the child to work at tasks beyond his years or ability. Nor should comparison be used to try to make a child learn tasks which any other child, regardless of age, can do with ease.

Rewards wisely given—and soon—are better than punishment for most learning.

# The Greatest of These Is Love

Before a child can learn, he needs to feel loved. The child who is loved learns more easily because he feels secure and happy with his parents. Then he learns to feel secure and happy with other adults.

A child cannot be given too much love. But to love does not mean to spoil. A gentle "No—I'm sorry. We do not do that" will give security to your child.

Children know that we love them by the way we speak to them, the way we look at them, and the way we handle them.

How a child feels toward people throughout life will depend, to a great extent, on how much he is loved in the early years of his life.

Yes—children learn more easily when they are loved by their parents and teachers.

# Putting Everything Together

If your child carried only his head around, teachers and parents would have no problems with him.

Isn't that a strange thing to say? Certainly.

But your child brings himself—his whole body. And sometimes it twists and turns and moves and wiggles. Sometimes it doesn't move enough.

Your child's whole body goes into his learning—how he feels physically, how well developed his emotions are, and how well he gets along with others. Educators know that your child's learning depends upon all these things: the intellectual (brain), the social (living together), the emotional (how he feels about himself and others), and the physical.

It is the desire of a wise parent to try to help his child develop in all these ways.

Be a wise parent! Help your child put all of himself together!

# PARENT ACTIVITIES FOR
# HOW TO HELP YOUR CHILD LEARN

## Activity One — "Proving statements"

**Read these statements. Check (T) if true; (F) if false. Find the proof of this in your book, underline it and write the page number on which your answer is found.**

T F 1. It is best not to show my child pictures until she/he has seen the "real" thing. Page_____

T F 2. Listening is a skill of little importance in learning to read. Page_____

T F 3. Smelling and tasting are as important to learning as the other senses are. Page_____

T F 4. The most important way of learning is by feeling. Page_____

T F 5. For children, doing is learning. Page_____

T F 6. Children imitate and being a good model is very important. Page_____

T F 7. Very important things need to be repeated even after the child seems to have learned them. Page_____

T F 8. We should not admit it if we don't know the answers to our child's questions. Page_____

T F 9. A child's learning has its ups and downs; sometimes fast, sometimes slow. Page_____

T F 10. Your child should draw upon what she/he knows in order to help learn new things. Page_____

T F 11. Rewards of money and "things" are the best ways of helping your child learn. Page_____

*(Answers may be found on pages 2, 3, 4, 5, 6, 9, 10, 11, 12, 13, 11, 17 in this sequence.)*

\* \* \* \* \* \* \* \* \* \*

## Activity Two — "Reviewing your book"

**On the pages indicated, underline in your book answers to the following:**

Page 7     Ten ways your child may develop his/her fine muscles.

Page 8     Some expressions you may use to stimulate and inspire your child to learn.

Page 13    Two things you should check out if your young child's learning seems too slow.

Page 14    Five ways your child learns.

Page 17    Three good rewards that parents need to give children in order to increase learning and get desired behavior.

Page 17    Three results of too much pressure on the child.

Page 20    Four things upon which your child's learning depends.

\* \* \* \* \* \* \* \* \* \*

## Activity Three — "MIX-UPS"

**On the left side are words your child is saying. On the right side is the type of learning which the words represent. Draw a line from the words to the learning represented.**

| "What the Child Says" | "How Your Child Learns" |
|---|---|
| "Let Me touch!" | By seeing |
| "I do like you do." | By motivation |
| "Look!" | By feeling |
| "Mama, why?" | By doing |
| "This is fun!" | By imitation |
| "Listen!" | By being loved |
| "Plant a seed." | Through curiosity |
| "Tell me again." | Through movement |
| "I am happy." | By hearing |
| "Yum, yum!" | By tasting and smelling |
| "Let me climb" | By repetition |

\* \* \* \* \* \* \* \* \* \*

**Activity Four — "Evaluating"**

**The following are expressions often heard in the home. Indicate with an (X) those which you feel would make a positive contribution to your child's learning.**

( )  "School is lots of fun!"

( )  "That's NOT the way to do it!"

( )  "Let's go over this again."

( )  "Let's show your nice work to daddy."

( )  "Would you like to help me dust?"

( )  "You are too little."

( )  "Come quickly, and look at this!"

( )  "You have certainly done a nice job!"

( )  "It's too bad. You've tried that before and failed."

( )  "Your coloring is not as good as Dicks!"

*(Did you check six statements?)*

\* \* \* \* \* \* \* \* \* \*

**Activity Five — "Identifying ways of learning"**

**On the pages of this book are titles indicating WAYS your child learns. The following are statements by parents. Write the way of learning represented by each.**

"See the butterfly on the flower."  _____

"Let's walk and find some leaves with different shapes."  _____

"Why not read to your doll like I read to you?"  _____

"Let's see what smells we can find in the kitchen."  _____

"Feel the furry back of the kitten."  _____

"What fun it is to read!"  _____

"Listen to the rain go pitter patter."  _____

"How is the lamb in the picture like our dog, Spot?"  _____

"Would you like to plant a little garden all for yourself?"  _____

"Let's string the macaroni and make a necklace."  _____

"I wonder why the rabbit went in a hole in the ground?"  _____

"You may spend the night with grandmother when you learn to finish your work."  _____

\* \* \* \* \* \* \* \* \*

**Activity Six — "Role playing"**

**Read the following dialogue and list six or more ways Gerald learned from the experience.**

**Dad:**  You can have a garden all by yourself right beside my garden. Let's look at the picture on the seeds and decide what you want to plant.

**Gerald:**  Lettuce and corn. And I like pumpkins.

**Dad:**  O.K. Let's make our rows for the plants. Listen carefully. Take this stick and dig a row from here to there. (Dad shows him how). Great job!

**Dad:**  Open the package of lettuce first. Be sure to look at the picture. *(Gerald has trouble but Dad lets him try).*

Now you do like daddy and plant the seeds. You drop them in and I'll cover them with soil.
*(They work together while Gerald talks, obviously enjoying himself.)*

**Gerald:** Now let's plant the corn.

**Dad:** Let's look at the seeds. Feel the corn. It is much bigger than the lettuce seeds. And the pumpkin seeds are flat. Let's look at them, too.
*(They continue to work together and talk as they work.)*

**Gerald:** I'll have a garden tomorrow.

**Dad:** No, it will take a few days for the seeds to come up. But we'll watch it come up and watch it grow.

### Ways of learning:

1._____     4._____

2._____     5._____

3._____     6._____

\* \* \* \* \* \* \* \* \*

### Activity Seven — Evaluating Learning

**Mother:** Look Nicole, I see a pretty cardinal in the yard.

**Nicole:** He's a pretty bird.

**Mother:** Yes, indeed. He's such an interesting bird and so beautiful. What color is he?

**Nicole:** Red.

**Mother:** Good thinking! I'm proud of you!

**Nicole:** Can we feed him?

**Mother:** He can get worms from the yard and insects to eat now, but when winter comes we will need to feed him because he can't find food then. He may be looking for a place to build a nest so the mother bird can lay eggs.

**Nicole:** Build a nest?

**Mother:** Find the bird book and we will look for a picture.

**Nicole:** (brings mother the book). Will you read the book to me?

**Mother:** Sure. I like books. Reading is fun!

List several good learning principles mother observed to enhance Nicole's learning.

_____

_____

_____

_____

## Activity Eight — My Personal Commitment

Learning is the process of acquiring experience and information. This can be full of wonder and excitement and I can help by . . .

*(Check those things which you feel you would like to improve.)*

_____ Providing a warm and loving relationship.

_____ Teaching my child to love books and pictures.

_____ Reading to my child every day.

_____ Encouraging my child to develop curiosity early in life.

_____ Giving my child approval for accomplishments.

_____ Setting reasonable and consistent limits on behavior.

_____ Refraining from "pushing" my child too hard.

_____ Introducing my child to new things, new people, new experiences.

_____ Listening to and talking with my child.

_____ Showing my child simple things and talking about them.

_____ Providing for lots of constructive play.

_____ Being a good role model.

_____ Providing for more rewards than punishment.

_____ Remembering that my child learns some things quickly, others slowly.

_____ Hiding any disappointments or anxieties I have about my child's learning.

_____ Expecting my child to learn to do only those things for which she/he is ready.

_____ Guiding my child into new areas of learning.

_____ Encouraging my child to ask questions and wonder why.

_____ Expecting that my child will not learn all things equally well.

_____ Using television for learning but not as a "mechanical babysitter."

_____ Knowing that my child's emotions are also developing.

_____ Realizing that my child will learn more if she/he is stimulated and inspired.

_____ Helping my child get joy from learning.

_____ **Enjoying my child** each step of the way!

* * * * * * * * * *

## Activity Nine — "Feely Bag"

Place small objects in an ordinary paper bag. Use objects having different shapes, for example cup, saucer, spoon, large button, handkerchief, ruler, compact, pencil, cotton, rock, etc.

Blindfold your child. Ask him/her to identify the object by feeling its shape and texture. Compliment your child for correct responses.